CONTENTS

For your free audio download go to
www.panmacmillan.com/audio/FastCars
or goo.gl/tX9uMx
Happy listening!

Cars all around

Cars come in many shapes and sizes. There are tiny cars and long cars. There are electric cars and bulletproof cars. And, of course, there are fast cars.

SPOTLIGHT: Ford Thunderbird

Manufacturer:	Ford Motor Company
Famous for:	first "personal luxury car"
First built:	1955
Top speed:	120 mph (193km/h)

FACT ...

The American Dream is the longest car in the world. It is 100 feet (30.5 meters) long and has a helipad.

The tiny Peel Trident is just 72 inches (183 centimeters) long and 39 inches (99 centimeters) wide.

The first cars

Early cars looked a bit like horse-drawn carriages. They had big wheels, tiny engines, and they were very slow.

The Flocken Elektrowagen was the first electric car.

When cars were invented, most roads were rough tracks. There were no gas stations, so drivers brought cans of gasoline with them in their car. Drivers also had to know how to mend their own car.

FACT ...

When the first cars started driving on roads, a man with a red flag walked in front of them to warn slow-moving horse-drawn carriages.

Built for speed

Sports cars are built for speed. They have a smooth, rounded shape, a powerful engine, and wide tires that grip the road as they race around corners. Sports cars are exciting to drive, although they don't have room for lots of passengers and baggage.

GB AU06 KGF

The Lotus Elise can travel at speeds of up to 150 miles per hour (240km/h).

The Prince Henry
Austro-Daimler
was one of the first
sports cars.

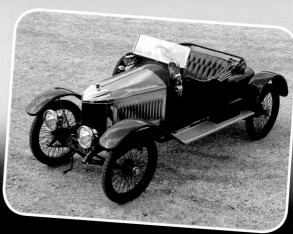

The Mazda MX-5
is the bestselling
sports car in
the world.

Supercars

Supercars are the fastest, rarest, and most expensive sports cars. They have an incredibly powerful engine and a very lightweight body. Only a few of each model are made, and each car can cost over one million dollars.

Bugatti Veyron Supersport: top speed 268 mph (431km/h)

FACT...

Supercars can drive at more than 250 miles per hour (400km/h).
That's as fast as a speeding express train.

SPOTLIGHT: McLaren F1

Manufacturer:	McLaren Automotive
Famous for:	fastest production car in its day
First built:	1992
Top speed:	243 mph (391km/h)

Hennessey Venom GT:
top speed 270 mph (435km/h)

Track racers

You can see the thrills and spills of car racing at a racetrack. There are races for sports cars and for special racing cars. There are even races for family cars.

Road cars race around a track in Istanbul, Turkey.

The drivers sit inside a strong cage that protects them in case they crash. They wear a fireproof suit and a helmet.

FACT ...

Racing drivers usually stop in the pits during a race to change the car's tires. Their team can change all four tires in just eight seconds.

All four tires are usually changed at the same time during a pit stop.

Formula One

The fastest race cars are Formula One cars. They are specially built for track racing, with top-quality tires and a low body to grip the surface of the track.

Formula One cars race in a series of races called Grand Prixes. At the end of the season there are two champions: one driver and one car constructor.

In a Formula One race, cars can reach speeds of 220 mph (360km/h) or more.

SPOTLIGHT: Mercedes F1 W05

Manufacturer:	Mercedes
Famous for:	Constructor Champion 2014
First built:	2014
Top speed:	estimated 225 mph (362km/h)

Formula One driver Jenson Button prepares to race.

Rally racing

Rally races do not take place on a race circuit. Instead, the cars race from one point to another traveling along muddy roads and dirt tracks, choosing their own route. Sometimes they race through the snow and over frozen lakes.

Some rally races go across the desert.

FACT ...

In the Dakar Rally, the world's longest rally race, cars can drive for up to 560 miles (900km) each day across sand dunes, rocks, grass, and mud.

The fastest car

The current land speed record is held by Thrust SSC, a jet-propelled, supersonic car. In 1997, fighter pilot Andy Green drove Thrust SSC at 763 mph (1228km/h) in the desert in Nevada.

New cars that could possibly break the land speed record are the Bloodhound SSC and the North American Eagle.

FACT ...

Thrust SSC was the first land vehicle to travel faster than the speed of sound.

Thrust SSC travels faster than some jet planes.

Spotlight: Thrust SSC

Manufacturer: SSC Programme Limited
Famous for: holds world land speed record
First built: 1996
Top speed: 763 mph (1228km/h)

Custom cars

Some car owners make their cars look weird and wonderful. They take off parts and add new ones, such as mirrors and wheels. Sometimes owners even change the actual shape of the car.

FACT ...

Drag racers use parachutes to slow down at the end of a race.

Some custom cars are built for drag racing. These are called dragsters. They race each other along a short track at high speed.

Custom cars are often painted with amazing patterns and colorful pictures.

Movie cars

Sadly, some of the most exciting cars ever made only exist in movies. James Bond's car, the Batmobile, and Chitty Chitty Bang Bang all have impossible extra features. When writers create these cars, they let their imagination fly.

James Bond drives an Aston Martin equipped with rockets and an ejector seat.

FACT ...

In the 2006 film *Cars*, all the characters are... cars!

The Batmobile has sophisticated weapons and special shields.

In the factory

Most cars are made in big factories. Machines press and fold sheets of metal to make a car's body.

Robots do most of the work in a car-building factory.

FACT ...

Car makers build more than 50 million new cars every year. That's one-and-a-half cars every second!

The body moves through the factory. As it moves, the engine, the seats, the doors, and all the other parts are fixed onto it. When the car is finished, it is tested to make sure all the parts work properly.

Cars containing crash-test dummies are crashed at high speed to check how safe they are.

Electric cars

Most of the 1000 million cars in the world run on gasoline or diesel. They pollute Earth's atmosphere.

Electric cars run off a huge battery. They are quiet and do not pollute the air, but they can't travel very far before they need to be recharged.

A hybrid car has both an engine and an electric motor. They use much less fuel than normal cars but are very expensive.

FACT ...

The most expensive electric car of all time was driven only once and then abandoned— on the Moon!

It can take about eight hours to recharge an electric car.

Cars of the future

What kinds of car will we be driving in the future? Believe it or not, flying cars and driverless cars have already been developed. Flying cars have wings that can be tucked away. Driverless cars use cameras and sensors to drive.

Aeromobil's flying car has an autopilot and two parachutes.

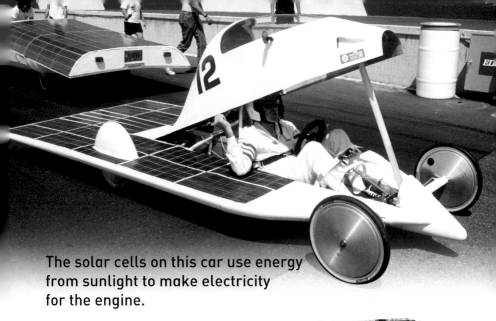

The solar cells on this car use energy from sunlight to make electricity for the engine.

Google's driverless car uses a very detailed map to find its way around.

FACT ...

It takes three minutes for Aeromobil's flying car to transform from a car into a plane.

GLOSSARY

atmosphere The layer of gases around Earth (or around any planet).

constructor A person or company that builds something.

crash-test dummy A life-sized doll used to see what might happen to people in a car accident.

custom car A car that is one of a kind because it has been built to order or has been changed in some way.

diesel A type of fuel used in some cars.

engine The part of a car that makes it move.

fuel A liquid that burns inside an engine.

hybrid car A car that uses both electricity and fuel to run.

jet-propelled Something that is moved along by a jet engine.

land speed record The record for any vehicle traveling along the ground.

motor A machine that spins to provide movement. An electric motor changes electricity into movement energy.

parachute A large piece of cloth joined to thin ropes. It slows down dragster cars and people who are falling from a plane.

pits A special area at a racetrack where cars stop to have their wheels changed and fuel topped up.

pollution Waste that humans put into the environment. Gases from car engines are one kind of pollution.

production car A car that is mass produced in a factory for general use on the road.

rally A long-distance car race that often passes through places where it is difficult to drive.

recharge To refill a battery with electricity when the battery has run down.

INDEX